Dearest ,

FOUNTAIN OF CREATIVITY

Ways to Nourish Your Writing

Thanks for all your

love & support.

love,   Jon

Bethany

`xxx`

FOUNTAIN OF CREATIVITY:

Ways to Nourish Your Writing

Bethany Rivers

www.victorinapress.com

Fountain of Creativity
Ways to nourish your writing

© Bethany Rivers 2019
First published in Great Britain in 2019
by Victorina Press
Adderley Lodge Farm,
Adderley Road,
Market Drayton, TF9 3ST,
England

Typesetting and Layout: Heidi Hurst
Cover Art and Design: © Fiona Zechmeister.
Art Work by Hannah Hull

*British Library Cataloguing in Publication Data
A catalogue record for this book is available from the
British Library.*

ISBN: 978-1-9993696-0-6 (paperback)

Typeset in 11pt Minion Pro
Printed and Bound in the UK by 4edge Ltd

This book is dedicated to everyone who has the desire
to write. It's not an easy journey, but it can be
a lot of fun.

May you find the inspiration, nourishment,
playfulness and cheerleaders you need, to help you
along your writing paths.

Contents

I Never Have Time to Write!

What gets in the way of writing? Life? Family? Children? Parents? Dogs? Travel? Work? Technology? Horses? If you have a story you're burning to write, you must write it. This means you have to make the time for it and make it a priority in your life. More about this in the chapter The Way It Is.

But even when you've done that, and you've got the morning to yourself, the kids are taken care of, you've got the morning free from all other work, free from commitments, free from interruptions, you have one last remaining hurdle, which is actually the biggest hurdle: yourself.

How do you get out of your own way and face down that blank page and *begin*? How do you do that? And when you begin, how do you continue? And when you've done that, how do you finish? In fact, the whole thing's just too complex, too intimidating and too much!

So, just forget the whole thing and go back to the beauties and stresses of the rest of your life. And let that poignant story, that insightful poem, that play on heartstrings, that moving script, that connective novel, eat and eat away at you from the inside until you are devoured and irritable and wasted without realising why.

Maya Angelou said that there is no greater agony than carrying the weight of an untold story inside you, and she's right. Stories demand to be told, they will knock on your door for years and, if you don't listen, they'll turn you sour. Be warned!

Creativity is one of the greatest health benefits there is. (Shame we don't reward it more in our society and promote it more in our schools – but don't get me started on *that* rant!)

So, what do you do with your lovely new notebook and pen or your laptop? You could run away screaming and pretend you never wanted to write, but your inner truth-teller will never believe you. You could go on a writing course, join a group, gain a qualification and these would all help. At the end of the day, you still have to face the blank page alone. But you don't have to do it unprepared – and that's where this book comes in.

Here you will find tools, discover secrets and experience the emotions and processes of other writers. Know two things: 1) *All* writers go through this, throughout their whole lives. 2) *You* can do this!

You will discover your own precious, exciting, frustrating, inspiring and fascinating journey of creativity. This is the book that is your lamp in the dark. Hold it up, read it well, take the next step. It will show you a myriad of ways forward.

> *'Whatever you're meant to do, do it now.*
> *The conditions are always impossible.'*
> Doris Lessing

As a writer, what do you need to do? Stephen King says: read, read, read! Write down the bones, Natalie Goldberg tells us. Bird by bird, Anne Lamott says. Walk, sit, write, Goldberg also advises. Morning pages, says Julia Cameron.

And they're all correct, and many more besides. And then it's just you and the blank page. This is where it's all up to you. But you are not empty-handed, as you might think. You have a host of stories inside you, stories that have been growing since childhood, all the nursery rhymes, fairy tales, Enid Blyton, Roald Dahl, Arthur Ransome, Greek myths and legends, and much, much more.

You have all the books you've ever read since then, and all the films you've ever seen, and all the stories of your own life you've told friends and family, and all the stories you've listened to on the radio at bedtime, in the kitchen or whilst driving. You're chock-full of ideas and voices. We all are. And that's a good thing. All stories overlap and touch each other.

Shakespeare got his stories mostly from other sources. Religious stories are more ancient than we know. Story is how we make sense of the world, how we relate to one another and how we connect across space and time. The renowned poet Muriel Rukeyser said that the universe is not made of atoms: it's made of stories.

So, you already have an inherent sense of story if you read, watch, listen. And this is invaluable! And nobody has shown us how story works better than Joseph Campbell and nobody has illuminated Campbell's work on myth and story like Christopher Vogler in The Writer's Journey: Mythic Structure for Writers.

But we'll come back to this concept later. First of all, let's deal with the biggest monster, the biggest hindrance: self-doubt. Don't worry, there are lots of fun ways of dealing with this one!

Self-doubt goes something like this:

- You could never write like her, so don't even bother!
- You've got nothing original to say, so don't even try!
- This is all rubbish!
- Nobody would ever want to read this!
- What do you think *you're* doing? Who are *you* to write?!

… ad infinitum!

This voice can be relentless. How do you write through this diatribe of inner criticism? How do you drown out this cacophony of negativity? Feel the fear and to it anyway, Susan Jeffers advises. Your hand is trembling. Let me steady that for you.

Have pen and pad with you *everywhere* you go. Keep one in the bathroom – this is a good place to catch words!

Standing in a supermarket queue, get the pen and pad out, make some notes of what you observe around you or write down your current thoughts. Use a digital voice recorder or record on your mobile the ramble of thoughts, ideas and images that are careering around in your head.

How do you find your own voice? Now listen up, because Golden Rule #1 is the most important rule ever and is one that you will need to come back to again and again and again in the writing process. It's the foundation of finding enthusiasm, momentum and all those blasted words you've been waiting all your life to write.

Learn to be playful again. Give yourself permission to write total nonsense. It's liberating. Totally freeing. Just write *anything*. Free write! It can be ad hoc, a list, a jumble – it doesn't matter. The most vitally important thing is go and grab some words. Being playful breaks down the barriers, by-passes your inner-critic and gives you lift off!

In playful mode, you get dirty in the sandpit, you mine the coal from the pits, you dig up words from the clay of the earth so you can mould and sculpt them later. You can't create a story, poem or script without the words. You can't dig up gems without a lot of soil and rock.

Go play. Go get your clay. You can edit to your heart's content, later – *later*. For now, just go catch some words, any old words will do. Go be a dream catcher and catch dreams!

GOLDEN RULE #1
PLAY

Permission to Write Anything

So you've discovered that playfulness is key. And when you're playing, you have breakthroughs – the magic happens. Magic doesn't happen when you're over-analysing or kicking yourself to death over not writing a single syllable.

It's vital you remember to grant yourself permission, over and over and over, to write the biggest load of claptrap ever! Being willing to write badly is of paramount importance in the writing process. Getting the pen moving or the fingers typing is the warm up to the marathon. Warming up is essential! You can't expect to enjoy the scenery of the mind (the trees and moonrises) if you don't flex those writing muscles first. Otherwise you'll only get cramps and go into paralysis. Let your first words be a kind of limbering up – don't expect anything very much from them. They are meant to be preparation, not perfection. Ask any runner how much training and warming up they do first, before entering a race.

TRY THIS: Open a book at random (preferably a novel, short story anthology or a poetry collection, but a magazine could work too) and select the first few words or phrase your eyes fall on. Now WRITE non-stop, don't stop typing, don't stop the pen moving, for THREE WHOLE MINUTES!

Timing it helps. A lovely three-minute burst – everyone can do that, right? Right. And just keep those words flowing, even if you repeat yourself. It doesn't matter. It doesn't have to make sense either. The point is to free yourself from the immediate negative diatribe that comes up every time you try to write. This works. Trust it. Go!

Wanting to write the perfect poem, the stunning story, the dazzling dialogue are great desires to have, but they can also be the biggest obstacles to you actually getting any words down at all.

Go ahead, write complete drivel – that's great! Give yourself permission to do that. Out of drivel, great things come. You can't edit the words if you haven't got the words in the first place. Write anything at all, write a load of rubbish – edit later, edit brilliantly.

All writers, no matter how experienced or how published they are, write a load of drivel as part of their first drafts. That's perfectly normal. It certainly does not come out perfect first time, or even the tenth time! But you have to dive in and go get those drivelling words in order to refine them, shine them and polish them later.

No words = no polishing = nothing to show. Accept it. Writing a load of baloney is part of the course. There's no avoiding it. No escaping it. So you may as well give yourself permission to write any old nonsense that comes out. This technique bypasses your inner-critic nicely. You can always come back to what you've produced later with a fine-tooth comb.

This is an invaluable rule that has helped me countless times. It gets you started, gets you going. And when you totally accept that it's OK to write rubbish, it makes everything so much easier and lets things flow. It's when we hold on too tight to the idea of perfection that we strangle the writing process. The throat constricts, and words fail to appear. You feel like you're floundering in a desert, desperately searching for an oasis. The more you search and clamber for the perfect palm tree with the perfect pool of clean water, the more sand dunes you find. The way to let the words flow, to moisten your mouth and release your voice, is to know that any old detritus is acceptable. Accept the gritty puddle. Accept the unrefined sand dune. Once you have the words, any old words, misshapen and strange as they are, you can sieve the sands and filter the waters as many times as you like.

That's what editing is for, thank goodness.

GOLDEN RULE #2
IT'S GOOD TO WRITE NONSENSE

Nourishing Your Inner-Sweetheart

Right, it's time to overcome your inner-critic. Time to stop the monkey mind. Time to stop your inner-editor getting out of control. The only way to really flourish in your writing is to develop a different kind of voice inside you. As Natalie Goldberg says, 'develop a sweetheart inside you' – the voice of the nurturer, the encourager, the one who supports you unconditionally and cheers you on, just like a loving parent with their child. Then your writing can grow.

So, having actually written something, then what? You're more than likely still plagued by doubt. It's all you can do not to screw your writing up into a tight ball and play basketball with it, with the bin as the hoop. Should you show it to someone? They might laugh or criticise. Although, the thing you don't consider is that they might like it, admire it, connect with it, resonate with it. Even so, you're not sure if you've really got anything to say after all. The thing is to keep going, in spite of these thoughts. Keep writing anyway.

And don't throw anything away. This is the coal at the coalface remember. There will be gems, especially if you keep going. More about this in the chapter Throw Nothing Away.

The thing is not to let ourselves drown in the words of our inner-critic. So how do you go about doing that?

TRY THIS: *Get some coloured paper or some coloured pens (or type in a different colour, though it's more visceral if you write by hand.)*

Imagine a ten-year-old child. This could be your younger self, a child you know or one that is entirely made up. They come to you and say they've just written something but are too scared to show it to anyone for fear of being judged. Their biggest passion in life is to grow up and be a writer. But they're not really sure if what they write is any good.

As an enthusiastic and supportive friend, teacher, parent or guardian, if you had to write a letter to this youngster, waiting to bud, waiting to grow, what would you say to them? The child is waiting with upturned face, expectant eyes and a trembling hand. (If you find it difficult imagining a child, you could always try picturing your best friend coming to you saying they want to write, but don't think they can. What would you say to them?)

For at least eight minutes, just free flow a letter to them and don't stop writing. Eight minutes is good, because it pushes you past the comfort zone of five minutes, yet stops you from trying to pad things out too much in order to get to ten.

Don't come back to the book till you've done this. No cheating. Off you go. Do it now!

OK, done that? Excellent! Well done! Now you have in front of you a kind, supportive, encouraging letter in which you reassure that little one that they're doing alright – in fact, that they're being brilliant. They're going to go on and create beautiful things. Well done you.

This is your inner-sweetheart's voice. You've just connected with it big-style. It's so much more powerful if it comes from you, from within you, and not from someone else. You can disbelieve all the positive things others say to you, forever and a day, but if it comes from *you*, you recognise it as real, authentic.

It's easier to think of lovely and encouraging things to say to somebody else and much harder to get in touch with that voice for yourself.

You might want to go back and address that letter to yourself, type it up, frame it, hang it somewhere you can see it whilst you write. This is your authentic, never-runs-dry spring of reassurance, your inner-sweetheart or inner-cheerleader, who's always there, believing in you, even on dark days. You might like to repeat this exercise periodically to offer further encouragement and praise as you learn more about yourself and your writing process. See the Appendix for examples from some of my students.

An extra fun thing to do is to actually address the letter to yourself, put it an envelope with a stamp on, give it to a trusted friend and tell them to post it to you in two months' time. You'll have forgotten all about it by then, and you'll receive a lovely surprise in the post that will cheer you up and remind you to keep going in a very special way.

Repeat as often as you like.

GOLDEN RULE #3
DEVELOP YOUR INNER-SWEETHEART

The Writerly Self

Who are you as a writer? What are the different aspects of the person you are? What informs the make-up of you as a writer? And do these facets interact with each other? There's an insightful poem to help us uncover this wisdom, by Jalal al-Din Rumi, a thirteenth-century Sufi poet.

'The Guest House' is one of Rumi's most famous poems, in which he describes the human experience. He says that every emotion that comes to visit, whether it's 'a joy, a depression, a meanness', is a visitor. You should 'welcome and entertain them all' and be grateful for the dark or negative emotions as much as the ones we feel more comfortable with. You can accept the 'shame' and the 'malice', accept all emotions as a 'guide from beyond'. Each emotion brings its own wisdom, a message about who we are, why we are, what to do next. It's one of the most powerful poems I know about self-acceptance.

Here is a fun exercise for you. There's a student's example in the Appendix.

TRY THIS: *Draw a big rectangle on a fresh piece of paper. This is the guest house. Divide it up into two or three floors, with a few rooms on each floor, with a few vertical lines. Give each one of these rooms a name. Each room helps or hinders you being a writer.*

Some rooms you may want to include are: the Muse, Room of Ideas, Inner-Critic, Significant Other, Cheerleaders, the Judge, Library, Play Room, Music Room, Nature Room, Insulter, Kindly Parent, Editor, Teacher, Inner-Child, Audience, Stationery Room, Meditation Room, Procrastination Room, Inspiration Room... The list is endless. Your Writerly-Self diagram as a Guest House will be individual to you. This is a magical house, and anything and everything you want is here, but do include things that trip you up in your process too. This is a way of opening a dialogue with those aspects you may not appreciate as much. As Rumi says, every emotion is a 'guide'.

Once you've drawn your house with all the different rooms, now choose one room that is a powerful enabler of your creative process, and choose one room that you think gets in the way of your writing.

Give yourself eight minutes to describe in great detail the room that you feel HINDERS you. Tell me what it looks like. What objects are in it? What colour are the walls? Are there any sounds? Or smells? Any other living or dead creatures in there? How big is the room? Are there any windows? What does the floor look like? Is it solid? Does it move? What does the door look like or feel like to the touch? Don't go back over it or edit it. Just keep the hand moving solidly for eight minutes and see what flows.

Have a breather. Then give yourself eight minutes to

describe a room in great detail that ENABLES you as a writer. Again, what does it look like? How comforting is it? What gives that comfort? Cushions? What kind? Be very specific in your detail. Does it have a revolving magic window of beautiful vistas of the world to look out onto? Does it play music or sounds that soothe or inspire? If so, what exactly is the music? Does it give off the scent of your favourite flower or perfume?

Enjoy this. Then have another breather.

When you're ready, I'd like you to enter the first room you described and have a conversation there. Interact with whatever is in there and be aware of what feelings come up for you. But you're not going in empty-handed. First, you're taking an object with you, something of great significance from the enabling room you described.

Choose your object first, know it in great detail. Visualise it in your mind, its texture, size, shape, colour, sound. How does it make you feel? Why is this object so important to you?

Now write for eight minutes about what happens in the hindering room, knowing that you always have a quick exit and that you have an object from the enabling room to help you. All rooms are there to help in some way. The Judge and Inner-Critic just want you to do your best and for your writing to be brilliant, it's just that they don't go about it in a very helpful way. Have a play. See what happens. WRITE.

GOLDEN RULE #4
BE GRATEFUL FOR ALL ASPECTS OF YOURSELF

Embracing Vulnerability

'Risk anything! Care no more for the opinion of others ...
Do the hardest thing on earth for you. Act for yourself.
Face the truth.'
Katherine Mansfield

Often, there is a particular story that is knocking on your door, again and again and again, and it won't go away. And you may have incredibly high resistance to this. The more dangerous a story feels to write, the more important it is to write. And these are usually the stories that are the most personal, that cut to the bone, and you think – I can't handle this! I can't write about this.

When you are at your most vulnerable – although it's incredibly scary because that voice is so true and touches a place deep within you – that's when your words will speak deeply to someone else's experience and touch their heart.

Connection between people's hearts – that's really the most valuable reason for writing, for sharing what you write. It's the thing humans crave more than anything – to connect.

'… when I speak or write from my most vulnerable place, that's when I have the greatest chance of connecting with your heart.'
Cheryl Richardson

It takes courage to write and even more courage to write something so personal it burns you to look at it. But that is the very story you most need to write and most needs to be heard. There's a lovely exercise you can do to initialise breaking down the barriers.

TRY THIS: *Give yourself five minutes. Write the sentence stem 'I do not want to write about…' and then keep the pen moving (or fingers tapping) and just see what comes. Keep using the refrain every time you come to the end of a thought, just write again 'I do not want to write about…'*

If you get into the flow of this list, feel free to go for another few minutes. Then reflect on it and see how you feel about what has come up. Are there any surprises? Was it predictable? Which of those things on the list feels the most 'dangerous'?

Choose the top three that you have the highest resistance to writing about. Spend two to three minutes on each of them, using the sentence stem 'I do not want to write about … because…' Keep going. Again, use this sentence as a refrain to keep going back to if you get stuck or come to the end of a particular thought.

These lists may bring you many insights. It might break the ice and give you a first line that you *can* write from. Or it might reveal to you the reasons why you feel you can't write about a particular topic at the moment. Remember, these feelings may well change over time. This is all about playing detective, self-excavation, bringing to light deeper thoughts.

Do lovely things for yourself. Provide your own security blankets during this exercise. That could be playing your favourite music, drinking a cup of hot chocolate or holding a gift from a loved one in your lap. Nurture yourself. Hear what stories are calling you. Listen to them. Let them write through you. Let them come up through your arm, into your fingers. Let your body's stories speak.

GOLDEN RULE #5
LET THE STORY FIND YOU

The Way It Is

In William Stafford's poem 'The Way It Is', he says that you never 'let go of the thread', that you follow this thread throughout your life, no matter what happens, but he never specifies what the thread is – that's up to the reader to decide. Even so, his imperative is that you do not *ever* let go of this thread. It's your guide, just as Ariadne helped Theseus find his way out of the labyrinth by unravelling a ball of thread. The thread can mean a myriad of different things, it could be: hope, love, curiosity, a loved one, kindness, inspiration... and the meaning may change over time.

If you've not been published, and we all start out that way, or even if you have no interest in ever being published, it can be very difficult to convince the people around you that what you are doing (writing) is valid or at all important.

It can be very hard to persuade those nearest and dearest to you to give you the time and space needed in order to write. This can be tricky. It can be hard to say 'no' to others when you want to spend time alone, writing. And it can be difficult explaining to anyone else what it is you're writing about when often you're not sure yourself.

In the poem 'The Way It Is', the thread never changes, and people keep wondering about what it is exactly that you're pursuing. Writing is an invisible thread you follow. Others can't see it, but you can feel it running through your hands, pulsing in your blood. It helps to know why you're writing something, even if you never articulate that reason to anybody else. But you don't have to. You don't have to justify your writing, though people who write often feel that they have to. Joggers don't have to justify why they run. Musicians don't have to justify why they compose. Artists don't have to justify why they paint. We don't have to justify why we write.

When I say the reason why you are writing', I don't mean any old reason, I mean the *deepest* reason. There will be a million and one different reasons. To become famous, to get rich – if they're reasons, forget it! That won't sustain you. Most writers don't become famous and most of them don't become rich either.

If you write for the love of it – great! What is it you love about it? Is it the playing with language? The total absorption of it? Is it to find out what you think? If you're writing because this story will just burn a hole in your heart if you don't – great.

Flannery O'Connor writes to find out what she thinks. Paulo Coelho writes to empty his mind and to fill his heart. Joss Whedon writes to give himself strength and to explore the characters he is not and to explore the things he is afraid of. Julia Cameron talks about writing being a way of claiming your world, of bringing clarity and passion to your way of living.

Knowing what your thread is, the reason why you keep writing, is what helps you keep going in the face of adversity. It keeps you writing when friends frown at you, or your partner rolls their eyes, or your neighbour doesn't see why you can't put that pen down and come and help them feed the rabbits that very afternoon. The thread is important.

It's your thread. Hold onto it. It's always there. It will see you through.

TRY THIS: *Brainstorm the word 'thread'. See how many different ideas, idioms and images suggest themselves. You'll be surprised how often we use the word in our phrases – losing my thread, weaving a story – and how many myths and folk tales contain thread – Ariadne's thread in the labyrinth, the three fates who spin the thread of life and decide on when you die, The Lady of Shalott. For five minutes write what the word 'thread' signifies for you. Go. WRITE.*

GOLDEN RULE #6
NEVER LET GO OF THE THREAD

Writing is a Visual Art

Blessing from Brigid*

"May your voice unfold like a velvet robe,
like foxglove leaves or heartsease. May your song
colour the hushing sunsets off your favourite coast;
feathering away the edges of the horizon.

May your ink-well be oak rooted: let your brush
dip and fly; susurrate in the swooping tail-flow
of red kites. May the wooden flute play
high luting melodies to cleanse your mind,

let the double bass vibrate, gyrate your hips
into figure of eights. May rainbows waterfall
through your thirsty heart, drink the cocktail
of sun and rain. May your mind be ignited

with lightning sparks. Come join the dance
of moonbeams and fire-fairies; daisy link your
ancestors to your new born in the dark: this

is the thread from which we weave
our songs of hope, of pain, and of poetry."

by Bethany Rivers

*Brigid is the Celtic Goddess of the Arts

Writing is not just black scribbles on white paper. Writing is not just your own vocalised voice set down in words on a page. Writing is a journey. And it's a journey made of images. If the words don't evoke images, then they're not doing their job.

Images are humanity's primary language. It's what the baby knows, before words. It's how dreams communicate with us. It's how films use metaphor and implication. Dreams also work through metaphor. Metaphor is a highly prized tool in any writer's toolkit. Metaphor works through the image, simultaneously on a concrete level and a symbolic level.

If you, the writer, are painting a series of cohesive mages in the mind of your reader – that's it, job done. Simple, eh? Interestingly, that's why poetry and painting are known as the sister arts and have long been entwined throughout the centuries. This is a whole genre in itself, called ekphrasis (Greek word, meaning to speak out), which is the topic for a book in itself!

> *'Painting is silent poetry, and poetry is painting that speaks.'*
> Plutarch

The way to let images speak effectively through your writing is through the use of the senses. And all good books on writing will tell you this, and they're all one hundred per cent correct. The use of not just sight (though obviously that's important) but what the characters can hear, smell, touch, taste. This is how we humans experience the world around us, so it *must* be the way that your characters also experience the world around them.

The reason you can't start to write your book, or write your story, with all those wonderful and crazy ideas swimming around your head all day for years, is that you first need to translate all those brilliant ideas into images. Images is where the language breathes and makes the characters and action come to life. No images, no writing. Simple!

Of course, translating your fabulous ideas into images isn't always easy either. Going from the abstract to the concrete is always a challenge. But this is where metaphor comes in.

If you write that a character feels sad, the reader is none the wiser. If you write about a character who is crouched in the corner of a derelict house, hugging their knees to their chest, the night surrounding them like the sea, then you've depicted an image of a very specific kind of sadness and the reader not only comprehends it, but experiences it.

If you write about a character watching a crow limping across a shaded lawn with a broken wing, that points the reader to another particular kind of sadness. This can also open out into symbolism, suggesting that the character also has a broken wing and needs to learn how to fly again.

TRY THIS: *Think of an emotion, any emotion, e.g. sadness, happiness, joy, boredom, anger, frustration. Marry this to an image, perhaps from nature. Then write for eight minutes, without naming any of the emotions at all.*

Show the reader what the character is doing, how are they displaying this emotion, through their actions and speech, or show it entirely through a description of location and weather (this technique is called pathetic fallacy). You could write the emotion through showing the behaviour of an animal, or a description of the room the character is inhabiting or wants to inhabit, paying attention to light and dark, colour and shapes, the spaces between things.

Have a play. WRITE.

GOLDEN RULE #7
WRITING IS A JOURNEY OF IMAGES

No Such Thing as an Original Story

*'Don't forget – no one else sees the world the way you do,
so no one can tell the stories that you have to tell.'*
Charles de Lint

It's really not what you write; it's the way that you write it.

You need to understand a couple of things, regarding the pressure of trying to be original. Firstly, there are only seven basic plots in the world (Christopher Booker: *The Seven Basic Plots: Why We Tell Stories*), so you'll inevitably end up writing one of these or a combination of these. Secondly, the point is not to write something original, but to find *your own way of telling* the story, your way of showing a story, discovering your own voice, your own style. That's the key. *You* are original. Your voice is unique.

The Seven Basic Plots are:

1. Tragedy – protagonist is a hero with a major character flaw, which is their undoing
   (*Macbeth*, *The Picture of Dorian Gray*, *Anna Karenina*, *Romeo and Juliet*)

2. Comedy – from confusion emerges clarity and a happy conclusion
   (*Bridget Jones' Diary*, *Sliding Doors*, *Mr Bean*, *Midsummer Night's Dream*)

3. Re-birth – an important event makes the protagonist change their ways
   (*Beauty and the Beast*, *The Snow Queen*, *A Christmas Carol*, *The Secret Garden*)

4. Rags to Riches – protagonist gains wealth (inner/ outer), loses it, regains it
   (*Cinderella*, *Jane Eyre*, *Great Expectations*, *David Copperfield*)

5. Overcoming the Monster – protagonist has to overcome the evil antagonist
   (*Star Wars*, *Shrek*, the myths of Theseus and Perseus, *The Hunger Games*, *Seven Samurai*)

6. Journey and Return – protagonist journeys to a strange land and returns with experiences
   (*Odyssey*, *Alice in Wonderland*, *The Wizard of Oz*, *Gulliver's Travels*, the myth of Orpheus)

7. The Quest – protagonist acquires an important object, facing many obstacles
   (*Iliad*, *The Lord of the Rings*, *Indiana Jones*, *The Land Before Time*, *Watership Down*)

TRY THIS: *Here's a fun exercise. Write in clear sensory detail your morning rituals of getting out of bed and getting ready to go to work. The more details the better. Eight minutes. GO!*

Try this with a group of friends, and you'll see how vastly different each account is, and how it's interesting and intriguing because of that. And you will never write like anybody else. And nobody else can ever write like you. And that's the beauty of it! You are already original. The way you write will be unique too.

If you wanted to take this writing exercise further, you could re-write what you've just got in the format of one of the Seven Basic Plots.

Think of your day as a Quest, and see what fun you can have with it. What's the goal? What obstacles get in the way? How are they overcome? Who are the helpers? What are the hindrances?

If it's a Tragedy, what's your fatal character flaw that undoes all your good intentions of getting to work on time? What part of you has to die along the way? Why does the character never accomplish their goal?

If it's a Comedy, what confusion will ensue, and how will it all be clarified and come right in the end? What masks are worn? What roles are reversed? How do things become clear?

If it's a Re-birth story, what valuable lesson do you learn? What rite of passage is fulfilled? What old things, old ways of being, do you need to let go of? What new things can then be born within you, within your life?

What treasures do you discover if it's Rags to Riches? Do you start from a place of poverty and discover some kind of richness? This does not have to be monetary. The treasure can be a new perspective, access to inner-love, a nugget of wisdom.

What monstrous mountains might have to be overcome if your day is defined as Overcoming the Monster? What dangers are there? These can be physical or psychological.

If it's a Journey and Return, what kind of adventure played out through your day? How are you any different at the end of the day from the start of the day?

Have fun. Have a play. Make it as mundane, surreal, eccentric, everyday, mystical, symbolic, as you like! Choose one, and write!

GOLDEN RULE #8
YOU'RE ALREADY ORIGINAL

An Object Tells a Thousand Stories

'*No ideas but in things.*'
William Carlos Williams

This is about letting the object speak for itself. A single object can tell multiple versions of stories. Where does it comes from, what does it looks like, what does it smells of, how does it feels in the hand, the weight of it? Where did the object originate from? Where has it been? What has been its journey? Who has it met along the way? How has it been passed from hand to hand? How was it made? What does it symbolise? What memories or associations does it evoke? What pieces of history does it hold?

Objects accumulate stories as they pass through many hands, get broken, are mended, thrown away, retrieved, displayed, treasured, destroyed, interpreted and misinterpreted.

In Margaret Forster's novel *Keeping the World Away*, you follow the journey of one particular painting by Gwen

John, from its inception by the artist, and then as it changes hands between a series of women, how that happens and what it comes to mean to each of the characters.

Objects are great stimulus to get the writing muscles working, get you deeper into a character's mood, behaviour or thought pattern, gives you something new to chew on, or get you to think about objects in a slightly different way.

TRY THIS: *Here's a fun thing to do whenever you're feeling a bit stuck: go to a few charity shops, bric-a-brac shops, antique shops. You don't have to buy anything, you can just look, touch and remember. Then have a think about what a character would keep in their pockets. Ponder what they would have on their windowsill. What would the character keep hidden in the bottom of their sock drawer, or under the bed? What can you show about a mood, event or character just though the objects that are present, and how they are interacted with?*

GOLDEN RULE #9
OBJECTS PROVIDE JOURNEYS

Replenishing the Well of Images

Creativity has its own natural cycles. Feel them. Respect them. Get to know them. Whenever we write, we are drawing on our inner well of images and experiences that have been assimilated, and ideas that have percolated through us over many years. Sometimes we dry up. Then we need to take a breather. We need to replenish the well. Stop writing for a while. Relax, go out and collect more images.

This could mean a trip to an art gallery, or going for a walk. Go camping, take up drumming, read something you wouldn't normally read, spend time with friends, go out into nature and take photos, create a collage, go to a concert, even do the vacuuming! Do something non-verbal: dance, paint, swim.

It could mean taking up a new hobby that has nothing to do with writing, preferably something physical so it gets your body moving, your energy flowing. Writers spend a lot of time stationary. The body needs movement to process things, to shift ideas and bring about new perspectives.

Here's a secret: non-writing time is just as important as writing time. And it's important what you do with your non-writing time. Don't spend it beating yourself up for not writing! You can consciously timetable non-writing time into a daily or weekly routine. Sometimes, non-writing time demands to be listened to, and the words just won't come. Don't panic! This is a natural part of the writing cycle.

Non-writing time is where you let in new thoughts, new ideas and new images so they can merge into old ones and help you glean new insights. Mostly this happens when you're not trying to do it. It happens when you're absorbed in other things. Everything in life feeds your writing. It's not an on/off switch. The unconscious can be very busy processing things when you're not looking.

Daydreaming is important. Give yourself time to do it. A writer is still working when they're looking out of the window.

It's important to notice when your well is running dry. Be kind to yourself. Do something nourishing for you. The well will fill up again. I promise.

GOLDEN RULE #10
NON-WRITING TIME IS IMPORTANT

Excavation of Personal Experience as Inspiration

'Fill your paper with the breathings of your heart.'
William Wordsworth

List the things you want to write.

Be fantastical – leave nothing out!

List the reasons why you write.

This may change over time.

List the books you love to read.

These are the kind you would probably like to write.

List your top ten favourite quotes on writing from other writers.

This is great fun and inspiring.

List the books/films you've loved/hated.

Helps clarify what you'd most like to write.

List the friends you can share your writing with.

Probably not that many.

List the ones you should not share with.

The longer list!

List the people who have had the greatest impact on you and how.

List the dances you would dare to dance

dance of joy, rain dance, salsa, dream-dance.

List the chapters you've written so far.

Chapters of life or your book or both!

List all the things you wish you could've said.

List the characters you'd invite to dinner/have executed and why.

List the songs of your heart.

List writers who have been rejected lots of times.

This is very cheering – everyone is on this list!

List your bucket list.

List your favourite flowers and look up their symbolic meanings.

List your favourite Goddesses/fairies/magical creatures and what journeys they take you on.

List your worst demons and what they're here to teach you.

List your favourite animals and look up their shamanic meanings.

List your recurring dreams, your daydreams, your night dreams, your life dreams.

List all the places you've been on holiday.

List all the places you'd love to visit/live, real or mythical.

List all the places you'd never want to see (again).

List non-writing activities that constitute great forms of procrastination.

List the transcendent moments of your life.

List all the things you can do during non-writing time that can nourish you.

List ten things that make you scream and the colour of each scream.

List your ten favourite words – write them big, in colour, and put them on your walls.

List your top three favourite objects, then write their stories.

List ten forgotten/lost objects, and where are they now and why.

List your childhood heroes and why they mean what they do to you.

List your accomplishments and failures – what changed you and how.

List ten different ways to play, then go play.

List five potions and spells you'd love to give to the world and why.

Choose a list and burn it.

Choose a list, type it, then frame it.

Choose a list, rewrite it.

Take the third thing from each of your lists and write them into one piece!

GOLDEN RULE #11
WHEN IN DOUBT – MAKE A LIST

What to Do When Feeling Down

Writing can be scary. Sometimes you're left to face your own greatest demons. Sometimes you fall into an existential despair – Why am I doing this? What is the point? – and sometimes a sense of lethargy or inertia can be a huge obstacle to your writing.

Listen to Mary Oliver's recording of 'Wild Geese' or 'Morning Poem'. Read 'What to Remember When Waking' by David Whyte. Read Sarah Salway's 'You Do Not Need Another Self-Help Book'. They offer wonderful invitations through words aimed directly at your heart, for you to feel that you belong in the world. Here's my response to Sarah Salway's poem:

One wish

the world has only one wish –

hidden in the roots of singing daffodils
whispered by skimming clouds
encapsulated by every rain drop
that slides down
my cheek

dawn and moonrise know the truth,
the multiples of single ripples
spread out on the lake feel it too,

blackbird and robin song, the breeze
of the grasses over hilltops, along the lawn,
every footstep and every heartbeat –

you belong
you belong
you belong

by Bethany Rivers
Published by *Sarasvati* (2016)

For some people this sense of belonging comes from
standing on a cliff by a great expanse of sea, staring at
a night sky full of stars in the middle of the desert or
countryside, sitting on top of a mountain, wandering by
a river, rock climbing, singing, horse riding, dancing …
It's that feeling of losing oneself into something bigger

than you, something amazing, something that holds you, nurtures your spirit. Nature is a great source of this. So is creativity, playful creativity, where there is no expectation and no pressure on any outcome or result.

Sometimes it means listening to some uplifting music, or going to see a fantastic show. It could be hearing your favourite poem read by a sensitive reader. Or rewatching your favourite film for the hundredth time. Put your favourite song on and sing along at the top of your voice.

Watch an inspiring TED talk on YouTube; I can certainly recommend Elizabeth Gilbert's talks on inspiration. Or a talk from Brene Brown on vulnerability. Or Cheryl Richardson's incisive life-coaching sessions. Read an uplifting poem. Learn a comforting poem by heart and use it any time you need it, as Kim Rosen suggests. Pick up the phone and talk to a friend and tell them you're feeling down. Share a hug, a good long hug, with a friend.

Read, reread and listen to John O'Donohue's poem 'Beannacht' (Gaelic word for blessing).

It's OK to put down the pen, switch off the computer and seek and receive comfort and reassurance. It's necessary. It's essential.

Get in touch with something that touches you, whether it makes you laugh, cry, sob or dance – and feel part of something bigger.

GOLDEN RULE #12
YOU ARE PART OF A BIGGER PICTURE

Thirteen Ways of Looking At ...

The American poet Wallace Stevens wrote the poem 'Thirteen Ways of Looking at a Blackbird'. This poem prompted many spin-off poems, such as Lesléa Newman's 'Thirteen Ways of Looking at a Poet'. You can have your own thirteen ways of looking at ...

This is a wonderful way of breaking through the thick ice of no-thoughts and lost ideas. Choose any concrete noun (or animal, real or mythological) and think of thirteen different ways of looking at it. Thirteen is a good number; it really pushes you to think harder and deeper about your subject.

You could also choose an abstract concept or emotion and list thirteen different ways of looking at that, one stanza for each way of looking. I've done this with anger and with love. And in each case, as I redrafted and refined the poem, it became less and less like a list. I deleted some of the stanzas I thought were too obvious or didn't lead anywhere and expanded upon others. The anger one, I'm happy to report, was published. (The first two stanzas are below.) But you'd never know from its final draft that it originated from playing with this exercise.

silence of anger

forks a tongue to sear
a new east and west
I pulled the duvet of silence

down over my ears
cotton wool of unmentionables
stuffs my mouth up

by Bethany Rivers
Published by *Obsessed with Pipework*
(2016) and *Amaryllis* (2017)

This exercise is fun and it keeps you on your toes. What more could you ask for?

GOLDEN RULE #13
THERE IS ALWAYS ANOTHER PERSPECTIVE

Finding Your Truths

The way to find your truths is not to scale the heights, but to dig deep: Seamus Heaney goes digging with his pen as his father digs the garden ('Digging'); Adrienne Rich goes down, down the ladder, into the sea, to examine the wreck ('Diving into the Wreck'); Helene Cixous advises that the steps on the ladder of writing go downwards ('Three Steps on the Ladder of Writing').

Why do we say write it *down*? When we're searching for truth, why do we talk about delving *deep*? When we want to get in touch with that voice of wisdom, why do we look deep *within*?

Fiction is the greatest way of telling the truth. And the best way to get to it is to go down deeper, delve deeper into yourself, down the ladder, deep into the depths, where the most authentic truths are. Going downwards encompasses the unconscious, where creativity springs from.

We think too much. We think creativity is about what comes out of our heads. We are forever consciously trying to articulate the story, the poem, the painting, the composition, but that is only the tip of the iceberg. What lies below the surface of the sea is everything else, and that's where the music and the poetry comes from.

One thing that good writers understand at a very deep level is that fiction is the best way of telling the truth. Fiction offers experiences of the emotional truth of living. Story shows you inside the hearts and minds of others. Poetry is a form of truth-telling. Story is how we share empathy. Myths are the maps of your own psyche and the collective psyche.

TRY THIS: *Write the first thing that comes into your head (or take a random line from a novel, a book of short stories or a collection of poetry and copy it down as a jumping off point) and then free associate. Just keep writing. And when you come to a pause in your writing, write 'but what I really mean is...' and then continue.*

At another pause, repeat that line, and see what you really mean beneath that layer, and keep on going, like peeling an onion, and just see what happens. Play.

GOLDEN RULE #14
YOU MUST DIG DOWN TO GO ON

To Plan or Not to Plan – That is the Question

Whether or not to plan, and how to go about planning, is different for each writer. Some writers need to have the whole thing planned out before they start. Some writers don't know what on earth they are going to write until they write it (like me!). Once I've made a plan of what I'm going to write, it's dead. The plan has killed it. Without mystery, I cannot write.

The only way you're going to find out what works best for you is to try it.

Try planning out a story and see how that feels. Whether that's just a skeleton outline, a chapter-by-chapter blow, in-depth character notes or a brainstorm with lots of post-it notes all over it so you remember to cover all the most salient points. Check in with yourself and see if the elements of the process are helpful or not.

Don't beat yourself up about it. There is no right or wrong way. There is no one way of doing it. If you feel the need to plan, plan. If you don't, then don't.

Have a go at diving right in there, and just write,

write, write and see where it takes you and how it feels to not know where the story is going, seeing the characters develop, letting the plot twist in front of your fingers.

How does that suit you? Does it leave you terrified and in a sweat? Does it cause excitement? Is it too much of an unknown? Or is the mystery what really makes writing a joy for you?

Dreaming is a form of planning. Never underestimate the power of daydreaming; every artist needs a certain amount of this in their life. It's dreaming that opens out the excitement of possibilities and the freedom of perspectives.

John Irving works out what his last sentence is going to be and then works backwards from there.

Some writers like to research the background of things first. Some like to do the research afterwards and fit it in around the story. It's entirely up to you. Only you can discover what works best for you.

GOLDEN RULE #15
LISTEN TO YOUR OWN PROCESS

Nobody Sits Down to Write a Book

If you don't believe me, try it. Go ahead – take a seat, your favourite one, in your living room, or study, conservatory or local coffee shop, with your best pen and pad or your laptop, and write your book.

Did your mind go completely blank? Did the view from the window suddenly become the most interesting thing ever? Did you think of a hundred and one other things you could be doing right now? Writing doesn't happen this way. All you're doing is intimidating yourself and asking the impossible. Stephen King puts it so well: 'When asked, "How do you write?" I invariably answer, 'One word at a time.' That's all we can ever do.

That one word may grow into one sentence, which may develop into paragraphs, pages, and may eventually, one day, become a book, if you're patient enough, persevere, and are kind enough to yourself about it.

And fall in love with it. Fall in love with those words.

Let the words lead you to a better phrasing, a better story. Let the words and the spaces fall through you and fall from what you love. If you don't love it, nobody else will either.

If you spend more time setting up a conducive atmosphere for yourself to write in than you do berating yourself for not writing, or not writing enough, or not writing well enough, you'll win. Set up that conducive space. Find out what that means for you.

It could mean walking where the trees are or by a river, eating delicious food or settling somewhere with a big table and a caramel latte, near a window that lets in lots of natural light. It means writing whatever comes to mind and not questioning it whilst in its first infant and intimate draft. (Questioning the draft comes later, after it's been in the drawer for three weeks. More on this in the chapter Throw Nothing Away.)

If you have very little time, carry pen and pad with you every single place you go, and if an image comes – write it down! Or repeat it over and over to yourself, if driving, until you can pull over and write it down.

Don't write a book. Write words. Don't worry about not writing. Go get some fresh air. Let your body move through the stress to a cleanness, so images can come through and write themselves on the paper or screen in front of you.

GOLDEN RULE #16
YOU CAN ONLY WRITE ONE WORD AT A TIME

The Contract You Make with the Reader

'… the introduction to a story makes a promise to the reader, says this is what this story is going to be about, here are the people to root for, here's the genre, the mood, the setting, the tone, everything. And then people read/view that promise and decide whether to sign on for the story.'

Jenny Crusie

You're always making a contract with the reader. You need to be aware what that contract is, and you have to be faithful to it from there on in. Otherwise, the reader will not forgive you. It works on the reader on an unconscious level as well as the conscious.

The opening offers the reader a certain kind of story, with a certain kind of character and a certain flavour to it. It's no good starting out as a thriller and then half way through becoming a romance. If it's meant to be a romantic thriller, then both elements need to be present from the start.

If it's going to be a violent and guttural read, make that clear from events, vocabulary or implication right from the start. Your reader won't thank you if they think they're settling into something comfortable like the cosy world of a May Sarton novel and then find themselves in the middle of a daring and dangerous Anne Rice narrative.

This is why the opening section of a novel is the hardest to write. (The end of a story or poem is also the hardest!) Go back to the opening after you've written the middle section, when you've worked out exactly what it is you want to say.

Any story offered is taken up by the reader on an act of trust. Make sure you honour that.

GOLDEN RULE #17
STAY FAITHFUL TO THE CONTRACT

The Process is Not Linear

The creative writing process is not linear. On a graph, the line does not go from A to B in an ever-lengthening straight line. The process happens in cycles, and you'll come across similar problems again and again.

Sometimes you may even loop back on yourself, then have a mighty leap forwards, then drop down again into a trough, then stagger up the next steep incline, then fall back again.

In Portia Nelson's poem 'Autobiography in Five Short Chapters', the narrator keeps going down the same street and falling down the same deep hole in the pavement.

By stanza five, she's learnt to go down another street. And I'm sure she will be hole-free for quite some time, but later down the line we all find other streets with holes in them that we keep falling into. This is a natural part of life. And it's a natural part of the process of creativity too.

Even Ernest Hemingway admitted that all writers are apprentices in their craft and never become the master. There are always new things to learn about every creative project you undertake.

So don't worry if you keep coming up against similar obstacles. Each piece of writing is new and will present you with different problems to solve, or old problems presented in new ways. All writers encounter problems to be solved in their writing – it's a continuous journey.

It doesn't matter how experienced or how well-published you are. With every piece of writing, you're pretty much starting again from scratch. But as you write more and accumulate more experience, you develop more tools to help you through the difficult patches.

GOLDEN RULE #18
THE PROCESS IS CYCLICAL

Sense of Audience

The very first audience you write for is you. You are your initial audience. Nobody else. You have to write what you love, what you enjoy, what engages you. If you start to think of other audiences too soon, it can become an inhibitor to the actual task of writing.

> *'You must write for yourself and not what you think people want to read.'*
> Jodi Ellen Malpas

When you are much further down the line, when you have your first full draft, then you need to think about who your reader is, that one person sitting down to enjoy reading your book: What age are they? What do they look like? What kind of films do they like? What tastes in lifestyle do they have? What gender are they, perhaps? What kind of hobbies do they have?

Then, when you're redrafting, you'll be able to keep the sense of structure and vocabulary cohesive, in adherence to the kind of reader you're envisioning.

If you find that you're being crippled by the sense of an audience judging you, and you find your words drying up, then reject this perceived reader completely, return to the sense of only yourself as the audience and let the writing flow again.

'Better to write for yourself and have no public, than to write for the public and have no self.'
Cyril Connolly

A note on writing groups: whilst a writing group can give you nourishing, constructive feedback, space and time to grow, a place to be heard, useful learning tools and confidence boosts, they can sometimes crush your spirits and can put you off writing for good.

Be discerning about what groups you join, who the people are in the group, what their motivations are. See how they treat people in the group, how respectful or nurturing they are. Ask the person running the group what guidelines they follow and if you can sit in on a session without having to show your work. Also, to state the obvious, if you're a poet, don't join a novelists' group, and vice versa. Ensure the group is one that can meet your needs as a writer, at the stage you're currently at. This will change as you develop.

Whatever you do, never write to impress others, to win approval, to win friends, to seek revenge, to become famous, to make lots of money. Write because you need to. Write because you want to. Write because you love it. Write because you have a story to tell. Write to stay true to yourself.

Eventually, if you want your work to be published, and

you've spent time honing and shaping your work, you'll think of the audience of an agent or publisher, which is very different again. Publishers and agents think about whether they can sell the work, which is a different kind of question from the quality of the piece of the work.

As well as the quality of the work, agents and publishers have lots of other factors to consider too: their budget, avenues of publicity, how well your work sits within the genre and style of taste they have, what books they've already agreed to publish that year, and what other projects they want to pursue or leave themselves open to.

Your ultimate intended audience may be just family and friends. You don't have to write for publication. Or you may just want to write the best piece of writing you can, for your own satisfaction. There are a million different reasons to write (so long as you don't do it for fame and fortune, as that rarely works out).

Write the truth. Write as if nobody will ever read it. Write as if you'll never read it again either. As Margaret Atwood says, 'You must see the writing as emerging like a long scroll of ink from [your] index finger.' Let the ink run, allow it to flow through your body and out onto the page.

But when you're writing your first draft, you want to stay true to yourself, true to the work, you have to forget about what anyone else might think, and let your own magic flow in your own private stream. So write about those strange thoughts, odd occurrences, unusual beliefs. Don't censor yourself. See what flows. Let the Muse have her way with you.

Don't worry about the first draft not being perfect. It never is. As Terry Pratchett says, 'The first draft is just you telling yourself the story.' The first draft is a journey of discovery. Second draft and further drafts are where you hone and refine.

Also, a word of warning about letting members of your family or your partner read your work – it's not always the best idea. They're not always your best cheerleaders! They might have their own way of doing things, or not understand much about the writing process. More about this in the 'Accepting Criticism' chapter.

If you are feeling nervous about your writing, always ensure that you can trust your immediate audience to be kind and reassuring or only give you the feedback that you request. You can always ask a specific question about your work and say you want answers to that only and nothing else. You're the writer. You get to say what feedback you accept and what you reject. Always protect your creative self!

GOLDEN RULE #19
WRITE FOR YOURSELF

Writing as Alchemy

'The true alchemists do not change lead into gold; they change the world into words.'
William H. Gass

Write to find out what you're really thinking.

Write to find out how you really feel.

Write to find out what the story wants to tell you.

Let the characters lead the way and show you how the story unfolds.

Before you begin to write your story or poem, take ten minutes to write out all the circular thoughts that are preoccupying you.

Things change as you write them. Things will take unexpected twists and turns. Allow this to happen.

Write the piece you keep putting off.

Return to the story or poem that keeps knocking on your door, even if you've written about it a thousand times before. An idea knocks on your door for a reason. It's telling you there is still some treasure here for you to uncover. Trust it. Go with it.

The conscious articulation of your writing is the tip of

the iceberg. The unconscious is much vaster, much deeper and more powerful. It knows more than you do. Let it speak.

Explore tangents – you never know what valuable places they'll take you. You can decide afterwards if you want to keep them, edit them or delete them. (Remember, don't totally discard anything. Keep these deletions in a separate folder called 'Shavings'. More on this in the chapter 'Throw Nothing Away'.)

Let editing be a new way of creating, a refining of the writing. It's like the decorating and honing of a clay pot. Your words are your clay. See what shape your clay pot wants to be, what spaces it wants to hold.

Writing has a wisdom all its own. And you can't tap into that unless you're actually writing!

Writing can change the way you think and the way you feel. It's magic! It's alchemy!

GOLDEN RULE #20
LET WRITING SHOW YOU THE WAY

Fountain of Creativity

In the powerful poem 'The Fountain' by Denise Levertov, the imagery speaks of the fountain of the heart. The reassurance of the fountain is always there and the heart can always be replenished. Likewise, Louise Glück in her poem The Wild Iris, speaks of the great fountain at the centre of her life, which helps her find her voice. A fountain is a very rich metaphor for the creative life. Other water words also fit: finding the source of your creativity, tapping into your images and inspiration, getting into the flow of it.

TRY THIS: *Brainstorm the word 'fountain' for two minutes. What comes up for you? Think of fountains you've seen, visited, heard of. There are many idioms with the word fountain in: e.g. fountain of knowledge. Myths and stories often have fountains. There are all different kinds of fountains: drinking fountains, chocolate fountains, etc. Free-associate, have a play.*

Then describe your own personal magic fountain of creativity. It can be based on a fountain you know or you can make one up. Describe it using the five senses. What does it look like? Is the sun shining? Is there moonlight? Are there unicorns? What kind of flowers or rocks are there?

What can you hear? Any birdsong? What does the water sound like? What can you smell? What surrounds you? Is it woodland? Beaches? Does anyone else know about this place? How easy is it to get to? What do you feel when you're there? How do you interact with it? Do you paddle? Lie down next to it? Bathe in it? What does the water bring you?

Describe in as much detail as you can for eight minutes. Go. Play.

You might want to find images on the internet to evoke the atmosphere of the place. Type up what you write, print it out, frame it, decorate it with leaves or objects from the beach or garden. Make this a special place you can return to again and again in your mind. It can become a regular ritual, spending ten or fifteen minutes at your fountain of creativity before you start to write.

This is your very own fountain of creativity. Enjoy!

GOLDEN RULE #21
THE FOUNTAIN IS ALWAYS THERE

Central Images

Go to one of your all-time favourite films, one you know really well. If you had to pick one image from the whole film, just one, that pin-pointed the essence of the story, what would it be?

The central image often carries the weightiest or most poignant moment of the whole story.

The central image is the one image in the story where everything leads to, or stems from. If you took this image away, the story couldn't exist. If every event in your story relates to the central image, you know you're on the right track, and it will keep you on track. You might not know what the central image is until you've completed a first draft.

If you looked at *Dirty Dancing* for instance, you might say the central image was where Baby is talking to her father, crying, saying sorry for letting him down, but that he let her down too. If you take this as a central image, let's see how this then relates to the start of the film and the end of the film.

In the opening scene, Baby is in the car with her sister and parents, and she's narrating that they're going away for the summer and, amongst other things, she states that she thinks she'll never find a guy as great as her dad. What follows from here is, of course, the love story between her and a dancer, Johnny, who her father does not approve of.

Let's look at the end of the film: Baby has had some harsh realisations about the nature of life; discovered more about her sense of identity; stood on her own two feet, stood up to her father, stood up for her lover; has (seemingly) lost both the loving relationship with her dad and lost her lover too.

At the end, Johnny reappears and says, 'Nobody puts Baby in a corner.' He then whisks her off up onto the stage, to show the world what great dancing really is. After all that (and discovering that Johnny wasn't the one who got Penny pregnant), her father hugs Baby and tells her how 'wonderful' she looked up there, accepting both Baby's new identity as a self-assertive young woman, and accepting the new love of her life.

You will find that every scene is related to this central image. It all leads to the growth of Baby, of her growing away from her dad, and becoming an adult in her own right.

Try it with other films. Play around with what you think the central image could be. Does everything lead up to it, or lead on from it? Compare the central image to the start of the story and the end of the story. What do you learn from this? Have fun. Play.

GOLDEN RULE #22
RELATE EVERYTHING TO THE CENTRAL IMAGE

Timelines for Everything

Some writers like to have their timeline of action in place before they begin writing, like the novelist Janet Evanovich. Whether you create a timeline at the start of the writing process or when you're in the middle of your plot, you do need to write a timeline. Possibly several: a timeline for the overall plot and a timeline for each character, so you can see how the timelines interact with each other. Keep in mind that only novels, memoirs and autobiographies need timelines. You don't need to create timelines for short stories or poetry.

Throughout the course of writing a book, timelines are essential. They keep you on track and keep you sane. They help you hold the entire story in your head. And they help you keep all the threads of the narrative alive and organised so you can see what they're doing and when.

There are software programmes that can help you create your outlines, like Writer's Café (www.writerscafe. co.uk). But often, the best way is to print out your timeline so you can see it all tangibly spread out before you, all in one go. Stick it up on your wall. And know that timelines are working documents, they are there to be amended.

A timeline is like a washing line, and you peg events onto it. Summarise each chapter into one short sentence. Write this on a piece of card. Place the cards in order. You can peg them on the washing line and swap the events around as and when needed.

A timeline can tell you what scenes or chapters you've written, which you are still to write, which ones still need editing.

You can do a timeline for each of your characters' lives and compare them to the timeline of the novel and display them on the wall.

Timelines are great for keeping tabs on time lapses, so you know that the seasons appear in the right order, the ages of your characters are in line with each other, and you can tell if a year has passed for one character and only a few months for another.

You have to have timelines clear in your head so the reader is not confused about what happens when. Unless you *want* the reader to be confused! Even so, the writer must always have an accurate picture of the timeline and be in control of it.

You may not know everything that needs to be on the timeline right away, but whenever you write a new scene or chapter, update your timeline. That way, you keep clear tabs on your writing progress.

GOLDEN RULE #23
ACCURATE TIMELINE = COHESIVE NOVEL

Too Much Emotion

Language needs to have a simplicity about it to the point that a child can understand it, and yet simultaneously it should have layers of meaning that someone of high intelligence can appreciate.

When there is no subtext, no implication, and the main message of the writing is written large and obvious, over and over, this is not good writing. The reader does not appreciate being hit over the head with a message, nor does the reader need things spelled out to them.

Let the reader fulfil their role in the completion of the process, let them work things out, fit clues together. They will find it ultimately more satisfying and the writing will be much more muscular.

If you want to write about a big issue, you have to pay attention to the smallest detail. If you want to write about the horrors of war, don't list the emotions of shock, denial and trauma. Show me some tiny detail, like a child's burnt doll laying in the road. The smallest thing sets up the biggest resonances.

If the main idea or emotion is made too explicit

and it's the one thing that is coming through above and beyond anything else, then it's really the author writing to themselves and telling the story to themselves, the one they want to write. The story is not yet ready for a wider readership.

There's nothing wrong with the writer trying to find out what their story is via this method, so long as they understand that's what it is, and that it's part of the process and not part of the end product. It's a very useful part of the process. Use it as such.

One red flag in writing is if you're using abstract nouns a lot (nouns that describe emotions and concepts: e.g. love, war, hope, hate, envy, justice). If you're doing this, stop. Think of an image for it instead. Let the image go on a journey. Let the reader feel the love, feel the horror, feel the injustice carried by the actions and implications of the characters interacting with one another.

Let the writing come alive like a series of images played out on a big screen, or through the physical embodiment of people on a stage. An actor doesn't say they are jealous; they act jealous. Show this.

'Writing is like driving at night in the fog. You can only see as far as your headlights, but you can make the whole trip that way.'
Professor Edgar Lawrence Doctorow

GOLDEN RULE #24
DON'T LET THE SUBTEXT BE THE TEXT

Not Enough Emotion

'Beauty without expression is boring.'
Ralph Waldo Emerson

Conversely, if there's no emotion at all being evoked by the characters' actions, and the writing comes across like an essay or a piece of journalism, and you never take the reader into the moment as it unfolds for the character, again, this is not good writing.

It's fine for some events to be reported, but if the whole story is reported, you keep the reader at arm's length the whole time, and you never let them see the minutiae of the characters' lives, it's all going to sound rather dull.

Reporting is when the writer glosses over the details and every event is seen as if through the wrong end of a telescope. The reader never gets to touch the texture of that character's life.

Perhaps the story is too big for you to write at the moment. Writers often skip over the important emotional moments – the very moments they need to stay with. If the topic is such a hot potato for you that you're scared of being burned, not enough time may have passed for you to be clear-headed about it.

It took me decades to be able to write about the death of my father. I know a colleague of mine couldn't write about Hurricane Katrina (the destruction and the aftermath) for many years, because she was too close to it.

So, if you're avoiding delving into the emotional lives of your characters, ask yourself what it is you, as the writer, are avoiding. The time will come to write about it. I promise.

For the word 'poetry', you can read in the word 'writing' in the following quote:

> *'Poetry is the spontaneous overflow of powerful feelings: it takes its origin from emotion recollected in tranquillity.'*
> William Wordsworth

Wordsworth is right. Creativity is the magical alchemy of deep emotion mixed with tranquil reflection. Remember that. You need both. And it's all in the timing.

Once you can write from that deep place, you've cracked it. (Sounds easier than it is!) Use the emotional avoidance as a way of flagging up that which most needs to be written.

GOLDEN RULE #25
UNLOCKED EMOTIONS TAKE YOU DEEPER

Throw Nothing Away

Don't throw anything away; just create another draft. Put the old draft in archives. If there's a lovely paragraph or phrase that you love but it *has to* go because it just doesn't fit, put it in a new file called 'Shavings' and maybe use it for something else in the future. A Shavings folder can become a storage space for future inspirations.

Immediately after you've written something, you might totally hate it. Immediately after you've written something, you might totally love it. Neither reaction is to be entirely trusted. If you throw it away, you may miss good coal that can fire you up later.

If you send your writing off straight away to a publisher, you may miss the opportunity to improve upon it. So, it's a good idea to put whatever you've just written in a three-week drawer. Put it in here straight away and *leave it*. Don't look at it again until three weeks have passed.

Three weeks is arbitrary, by the way. You can make it four weeks, you can make it two months. It's the lapse of time that is important. After time away from it, you come back to it with fresh eyes, a new perspective. Things will have happened in the interim, so you bring a different wisdom to it. The emotion is not running quite so high, so you can be more objective about it.

With new eyes, you can discern things like 'actually those sentences there are pretty good, it wasn't nearly as bad as I first feared'. You can discern that although the piece is solid, there are still some tweaks you can make, where it got a little sloppy.

It is said that you must kill your darlings. That darling phrase you've just written that you're in love with, or that stunning paragraph you're so proud of, or that chapter full of tantalising description.

You don't have to be so brutal. Just grow your awareness of what works and what doesn't. Those words that do not serve the purpose of your story or poem must go, but knowing that you can cut and paste phrases and words and whole chapters that may not work and put them in the 'Shavings' folder, enables you to be ruthless in the editing process.

The darlings don't get killed. They just get fostered out, or put in a drawer to go to sleep until one day they may be needed for some other important job.

GOLDEN RULE #26
USE THE THREE-WEEK DRAWER AND CREATE A 'SHAVINGS' FOLDER

Fundamental Fears and Desires

TRY THIS: *Interview your characters. Find out who they are, how they use their toothpaste, what they keep in their pockets, on the mantelpiece, which foot they use first to step out of the shower, whether they even like showers, what their favourite food is, favourite colour, most treasured childhood memory, the worst moment of their life.*

If you don't know the answers, ask the characters for the answers. Take one pen in your dominant hand and write the question. Take a different coloured pen or pencil in your non-dominant hand and answer the question.

Whatever the very first thoughts are, let that be the answer, even if the character is telling you to 'get lost'. You don't need to share any of this in the actual story, but your intimate knowledge of the character will naturally bleed into the writing, making it cohesive, making it convincing, making it whole.

Every character needs a fundamental desire and a fundamental fear. This underpins everything they do and say. Even if the character is not consciously aware of it, the writer needs to be.

When I say fundamental, I mean *fundamental* – not just the things your characters care about, but the things that absolutely *drive* them. The reader never needs to know exactly what that desire and fear is, but the writer certainly does.

If you don't know what makes your character tick, you've not done enough to convince your reader of three-dimensional characters. You might not know from the outset what your character desires and fears most of all. If you're not the kind of writer who makes a lot of notes or researches in great depth before starting to write, that's fine. You can write your way into it.

The mores scenes you write for your character, the more you get to know them. Accumulate that knowledge. Play the detective. Be on the lookout for clues. What is it your character cares about more desperately than anything else and why?

If in doubt as to what makes an effective fundamental desire of fear, there are some thought-provoking ideas in the Enneagram (www.enneagraminstitute.com). It's a clearly delineated system of the make-up, purpose and function of personality types.

According to the Enneagram (an ancient system, nobody is quiet sure where exactly it comes from), there are nine personalities, and although a character may have aspects of several of them, there will be one that predominantly fits. You don't have to believe in this idea, it just provides a useful platform to jump off from in order to create realistic characters.

There is no hierarchy, all the personalities have their gifts and their flaws. This makes it a wonderful tool for your ever-increasing writer's toolkit. For each of the personalities there is a stated fundamental desire and a fundamental fear.

If you choose one of these for each of your characters and then figure out how to show that through their actions, you're well on the way to creating well-rounded characters.

You may start out thinking your character's fundamental desire is to belong and their fundamental fear is abandonment and then discover later on, through having written much of your story, that their fundamental desire is something quite different, like avoiding pain at all costs. Be open to choosing and open to changing your mind.

Let your characters tell you who they are. Have fun!

See Appendix II for a summary of the nine personality types.

GOLDEN RULE #27
MOTIVATE YOUR CHARACTERS

When the Inner-Critic Gets Too Much

*'If you hear a voice within you say,
"you cannot paint",
then by all means paint
and that voice will be silenced.'*
Vincent Van Gogh

There are a number of fun things you can do to counteract the poison of a voracious inner-critic who stops you writing. Anyone who likes crafts or little boxes will enjoy this one. Get some squared paper (small squares). You'll need some scissors and some Sellotape. (Bit of a *Blue Peter* thing going on here!)

Draw a cross shape using squares as your segments and ensuring that all the squares are the same size. Cut around the full shape. Then fold along the inner lines, and you've got a cube! Tape the base together, but leave it so you can open and close the top.

(If you're clever at this kind of thing, you can create a fold-in flap. If you're not a craft-driven person, you can use

Blu-Tack or whatever you like, to make the box sealable and un-sealable.)

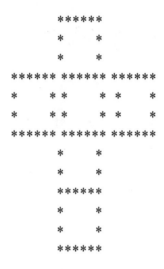

Create three boxes. Label one box Rampant Critic (RC), one of them Inner-Sweetheart (IS), (see chapter three) and one of them Constructive Feedback (CF). Colour them in. Decorate them. You might want to use lots of red for the RC box, lots of pink and green for the IS box and perhaps black or grey for CF box. Entirely up to you. They're your boxes.

Now, write down all the things you notice your RC says to you. Write them on little pieces of paper and put them in the RC box. When you sit down to write (or stand up to write), and you hear your RC tearing you apart, write down what it is saying and put them all in the box.

As you develop your inner-sweetheart, you might want to collect these in your IS box to reread and encourage yourself as often as you like. Quotes from other writers on the web can also be an aid.

'I once joked to a friend, "I've started writing a book. I'm doing really well. I've inserted the page numbers in the footer. I've inserted the letters 'xyz' in the header, ready and waiting for the title to transpire. I'm doing really well. It's only been six months since I started."'

Anon

The hardest box to get right is the CF one. These are neutral statements with no judgement attached. If there is a judgement involved, it's probably your RC talking. CF says things like: perhaps lose that sentence there, as it's a repeat from earlier; maybe delete that word there, as it doesn't seem to add any impact to that line; this paragraph needs to say where the character is, as the reader doesn't know.

The CF is a neutral observer who can point out things that need to be done in order to improve your writing. This is your invaluable inner-editor, who needs their own spotlight and time and place to weave their magic upon your words. But be warned, don't let your CF come in too soon. Remember to stay playful first, and go collect words, before letting the CF enter the building.

'There is nothing to writing. All you do is sit down at a typewriter and bleed.'
Ernest Hemmingway

Now, returning to your RC box, which will probably be the one to fill up the quickest, and may even already be overflowing with judgements and insults and barriers. This is to be emptied on a very regular basis. You can do several things with the notes that have accumulated. You can read aloud what you've written in a silly high-pitched voice. (Making the Rampant Critic sound silly disempowers it.) You can rip all the pieces of paper into shreds and bin them. Or you could have a ritual burning. Feed them to a small bonfire, or if you're lucky enough to have an open fire or log burner at home, feed it to that.

As you do this, you could speak aloud: say that you release the RC, you know it was just trying to help (not wanting you to make an ass of yourself, wanting your work to be perfect), but these things are actually not helping. And you can even do a dance if you like, to your favourite songs, and celebrate letting the RC go.

This may all sound very pagan, or hippyish. You can adapt this to whatever feels comfortable for you. The point to remember is to keep on being aware of when your RC comes up and is trying to sabotage your writing and then to actively do something about it, so you can free yourself up to write!

GOLDEN RULE #28
SOOTHE YOUR INNER-CRITIC

More on Originality

'Never change your originality for the sake of others because no one can play your role better than you.
Anon

'Originality is the by-product of sincerity.'
Marianne Moore

This chapter is a reminder, in case you forgot how your writing voice is just like your fingerprints:

Your voice is a golden thread

> Your voice is a golden thread
> a singular part of a world tapestry
> you are special already
> your voice is unique
> your song – the one waiting within you
> ready to be born
> is one of the threads
> pulsing in your chest
> waiting for your breath

your words
your tune
sing it loud
weave it in your colours
through the threads of others
without your thread
without your song
without your story
the tapestry is always incomplete
with a gaping hole
thirsting to be filled
and filled with only your gift
sing it
write it
it's yours and yours alone
no-one has a voice like you
no-one else can give your perspective
nobody sees things like you do
nobody experiences the world as you do
nobody else can weave
the thread you weave

by Cerys Griffiths

GOLDEN RULE #29
WEAVE YOUR OWN THREAD

Accepting Compliments

Many of us don't seem to be very good at accepting compliments. Especially women. The amount of times I tell my students off for not accepting compliments on their work …!

Here's an easy step-by-step guide as to what to do with compliments:

First step: Say thank you

Easy. Just say thanks. Even if you don't believe it, even if everything inside you is vehemently rejecting any possible nice thing someone could say about your writing. When you don't accept a compliment, you're throwing the gift back into the giver's face.

'Thank you for not thinking I'm weird. I mean we both know I'm weird, but you accept it, and that makes me happy.'

Anon

Second step: Park it

If you can't take in the compliment there and then, make a mental record of it to return to later, in a solitary quiet moment, and replay it. 'Oh, that person said they liked my work. They liked it. They liked my writing.' Repeat it to yourself many times. See how it feels in your body.

'You're the best person to hang out with because if I ask a ridiculous question like, "A hippo is chasing you, what do you do?" You'll say something like, "How big is the hippo?" And that shows that you're taking the question seriously, and I appreciate that.'

Anon

Third step: Treasure it

Write it down. Write down the exact words of the compliment. Type them up. Embolden it. Type it in pink. Or green. Or whatever your favourite colour is. Print it. Put it on the wall. Put it by your desk. Frame it.

Start a special book of collected compliments. Read and reread these in your darkest inner-critic hours, to help bolster you to keep going. At several times in your life, somebody else believed in your writing and told you so. Remember this. Draw on this.

Try this: *A compliment is a present. Imagine it in a box, wrapped in purple silk, with a big bow. You receive this standing in a beam of sunlight. As you slide the scissors under the bow and watch it drift to the ground, you feel that familiar frisson of anticipation.*

When you open the box, a warm feeling enters your heart and spreads throughout your whole body, like the sunbeam you're standing in. Keep this box safe, in a place you can easily find it. Open it whenever you like.

Or try asking for further clarification of the positive feedback. The more specific it is, the easier it is to take on board. If someone says 'that was the most brilliant short story I've ever read', it can be hard to accept. If someone says 'I cried during that part where your main character laid down next to her best friend in the barn to keep warm; the description of it really made me *see* it' then that qualifies the reader as someone who was paying attention. They gave a genuine response to the writing, and they actually pinpointed the exact part of the story or poem that affected them.

GOLDEN RULE #30
ACTIVELY LEARN TO ACCEPT COMPLIMENTS

Accepting Criticism

'There is only one way to avoid criticism: do nothing, say nothing, and be nothing.'
Aristotle

We can accept criticism all too readily, and unnecessarily! Whenever someone says something critical about the new baby of creation we have just proffered, it can wound deeply. I always warn students against sharing their work with their nearest and dearest as they can often be the most damning. Even by accident; the most innocuous remark can be damning.

If the writer's partner or family isn't familiar with the writing process and writing skills involved, their comments can be, to put it bluntly, useless.

Showing something you've written to someone, whether it's a friend, your spouse, your child, your best friend, is like handing a stake to them, lying down and letting them stab you with it by whatever words fall from their lips. You're that naked and vulnerable. And their words can be the guillotine, even if they don't mean them that way.

'Constructive criticism is alright though, isn't it?' I hear you cry. That depends. It depends on who has offered the criticism, and at what stage in your process it has been offered, and how in touch with your own process you are as a writer.

'Constructive' can cover a multitude of sins. And sometimes, it can actually prove to be constructive. What do I mean by constructive? I mean the criticism is *specific* and gives you something *positive* to work with, that the criticism doesn't just leave you paralysed by indecision, or burdened with a bunch of problems that you can't see your way out of, (like being trapped in a cat's cradle).

Criticism can say as much about the critic (if not more) than it does about the piece of writing in front of them. So, it's wise to be aware of what audience your writing is being aimed at. Check to see if the person offering their criticism is a member of your target audience. No point showing experimental poetry to someone who only likes the classics. If your book is aimed at nine-to-twelve-year-olds, ask a twelve-year-old what they think of it.

Don't unquestioningly accept criticism of your poetry from people who primarily read or write novels. Don't unquestioningly accept criticism from a friend or family member who has a different perspective of the same life experience as you. They will have their own story to tell. That's not the same as yours. Protect your own creative narrative.

> '*Criticism, like rain, should be gentle enough to nourish [your]
> growth without destroying [your] roots.*'
> Frank A. Clark

At the end of the day, you are the writer of your own words, and only you can tell, at the very heart of it, if a piece of criticism is of use to your writing or not. As the writer – you get the first and last say, unless you're getting published, then the publisher gets a say in it too!

You always have a choice. You can choose to take on board any criticism and work with it, or to leave it, ponder it, question it, discuss it, or totally disregard it.

> *'I pay no attention whatever to anybody's praise or blame. I simply follow my own feelings.'*
> Wolfgang Amadeus Mozart

For any egotists out there, constructive criticism (in the true sense), is of utmost importance. A second pair of eyes can offer more objectivity and insight than you yourself can when you're too close to your own work. This will be needed at some point in the later stages of the process, if you are hoping to publish. (If you don't want to publish or have anybody else make sense of your work, criticism doesn't really matter.)

Just be aware of when you're taking on board criticism, and what kind of criticism it is. Question how helpful it is, at that very moment in your writing, and what would best enable your writing to continue and improve. It is your prerogative to do so. It is vital that you do so.

> *'Do your thing. Do it unapologetically. Don't be discouraged by criticism [...] Pay no mind to the fear of failure. It's far more valuable than success. Take ownership, take chances, and have fun. And no matter what, don't ever stop doing your thing.'*
> Asher Roth

Also, you can direct the feedback you want. Ask a specific question to the reader or listener, before they encounter your work, so that it focuses their attention. Tell the reader or listener what you want. Tell them you don't want any comments at all at this point, you just want to see how it sounds in the air, how it sounds when you read it aloud to other people.

Reading aloud is always useful, especially in the early stages. Reading aloud by yourself to an empty room helps you hear how the words sound, if the rhythms work, and where the breath falls. (The breath needs to coincide with commas and full stops.) Even if you don't wish to receive criticism from anybody else, just reading it aloud to another pair of ears, without them making any comment at all, can be very useful. The very act of your words being spoken aloud to a new set of ears helps you discover which parts of your writing flow and which parts don't make sense, and which words stumble over each other.

On the other side of the coin, if you have been sending work out to publishers and you keep getting rejections (remember that all writers receive way more rejections than acceptances), it is worth seeking advice from an experienced writer and tutor. They may very well be able to shine a light on your work, where you could not. Feedback from the right person can be absolutely invaluable.

So, yes, of course, criticism is needed, and it can be very useful and make you a better writer. But – ensure that you trust the person who is offering their criticism. Check if they are coming from an experienced (writerly experience) place from within themselves.

Other questions to think about: Are they affiliated to the kind of audience you're aiming at? Are you in a place within your process where this kind of feedback would be useful? Are they coming from a benevolent intention in wanting to see your writing flourish?

Remember, you always choose how much to take on board and what to do with that criticism. Own it, or reject it. It's up to *you*.

GOLDEN RULE #31
BE DISCERNING OF YOUR CRITICS

You Didn't Want to Hear This!

You're always a beginner. No matter how much you write and how much experience you gain, whenever you start a new piece of writing or a new writing project, you are a beginner again. This is because every book, every poem, every story, requires something slightly different from us; each of them is an individual child with different needs.

What you glean from your experiences as a writer are more tools to help you solve the ever-emerging riddles. The more you write, the more you learn. For published writers, who have been published many times, each new project still brings its own insecurities, doubts and problems to solve. However, they've had more time to get to know their own writing process, have a better chance of persevering, have a greater amount of patience and more tools in their kitbag than someone who is less further along the writing road.

This is not the bad news you think it is. It's a great release, in fact, that frees you up to be ever more creative! It means you can return to Golden Rule #1 – PLAY.

Remember earlier – we talked about the process not being linear. The creative process is like a snake eating its own tail: every beginning leads to an ending and every ending leads to another beginning.

GOLDEN RULE #32
YOU ARE ALWAYS A BEGINNER, JUST A MORE EXPERIENCED ONE

APPENDIX I
LETTERS FROM INNER-
SWEETHEARTS

Dear Young Geraint,

Realise that this impulse inside you to write is natural, legitimate and beneficial. Give it the space to grow without concerning yourself about *how* it will grow.

Resist thoughts that suggest it might be self-indulgent to want to write or that it is born of pretension. The impulse is as normal as the urge to run or play football. Look after your writing muscles and they will very likely grow stronger and help keep your creativity active throughout your life.

You are coming across poetry at school and reading scholarly criticism of that work. Don't be intimidated by what is written about poetry and try not to think that there is an intellectual benchmark that must be attained for poetry to be legitimate.

It might be helpful to think of poetry not as coming from you but as coming through you. That you are a conduit for its expression. This might help you to resist judging what you write.

Above all enjoy your poetry and the birthing process that gives it life. Be glad that you are able to create something out of your experience of the world.

Do not be embarrassed about your poetry and what it might reveal about you.

Share it with whomever will listen.

Yours encouragingly,

    Geraint

* * *

Dear Young Bethany,

You don't know this yet, but you are already a poet.

It's not about whether you've written anything or not, and it's not about how 'good' your writing is. (You'll discover Clarissa Pinkola Estes, who will point the way.) It's a way of being. A way of looking at the world. A way of approaching life. It's hard to define, but you already have it. It will be many years before you see this reach the light of day. But know that you are a poet, this essence is within you. It is a gift, even if it doesn't always feel like so.

Poets have the power to dig deep to find the words and so be a light for others in times of darkness. You have this. (You'll discover Adrienne Rich and Jeanette Winterson, who will show you this.) It will take time to discover this about yourself, say another eighteen years of reading, experiencing, observing, learning, teaching, feeling, reflecting, longing. But time is a nonsense anyway, so don't worry about that.

The thing is, poetry is your thread. (As William Stafford will inform you.) You may lose it from time to time, for long periods of time, and that's OK. Just remember, it is always there, even when you can't see it, just like the stars are always there, even during the day, and your friends are always there, even if they're living in a different county, another country.

Although sometimes you may be afraid that poetry has deserted you, poetry will return to you, again and again. (Like Pablo Neruda says.) You may fall out with it sometimes, get frustrated with it, even angry with it at other times, but it will find you again, with another peace offering, a new perspective. It will reveal images and narratives of healing, inspiration, truth. And in turn, once you've digested it, you are fully capable of offering these poems to others, for them to explore their truths, find their inspirations.

Remember the path of discovery of your poetry and others' is not linear. It's cyclical. It begins and begins again.

Though you may sometimes be afraid of the truths poetry reveals to you, remember it is an access point to your own inner wisdom. Lean into it. Let it guide you.

And never be afraid to write bad poems. All poets do. It's part of the course.

Don't keep running after inspiration though – that's the key. Let yourself be receptive. Remember to keep playing. And when you need time out – learn to recognise that, and it will reward you. Let poetry find you, love you in its own way.

Wishing you a deepening journey into the many languages of poetry,

Love from Bethany

* * *

Dear Young Denise,

I have read some of your stories and I know you are very good at writing. I want to tell you to keep on writing. Don't ever give up because you think you are not good enough. You have so many stories to tell and as you grow older, life will take you on a journey where each and every day you will have new experiences to write about. You will go to new places, meet new people. You will see, touch and hear so many things.

The desire to write is a spark inside you. Be careful, be very careful. Don't let it be blown out by other people's belittlement, derision and scorn. Nurture that spark. Guard it, build a strong fortress around it to protect it from those negative voices. For if you listen to those voices long enough, you will wake another voice, one that also lives inside you, like the spark. Beware, beware for he is a very nasty, destructive, vengeful voice that tells you, 'You can't do this.'

The spark, surrounded by its fortress, can't be allowed to hear that voice. If it listens to it, it is in danger of dying away. This is what you need to do with your spark. Feed it. Feed it every day and watch it grow bigger. Here are the instructions for feeding your spark.

1. Honour your spark. You can do this by always carrying a pen and notebook. Often something you see, an observation you have, will cause your spark to glow more brightly. Quickly jot down your observations. Your spark can build a fire with them later by developing them into stories.

2. Write your stories and don't worry about spelling and grammar, they will get in the way of your flow. You can always look at that later.

3. Read, read, read as much as you can. Your spark loves to hear about the adventures and antics of others. When you are drawn into someone else's story, your spark goes with you. Often it experiences so much wonder and excitement that it bursts into flames.

4. Find someone you trust to read your stories to. Be careful though, some people do not understand the spark that is within you. They may decide to give you advice and their words could inadvertently pour cold water on your spark and put it out completely. If this happens, don't worry, take your spark back to the fortress and bring it back to life by following any of the above steps.

By carrying out these instructions, you will nurture your spark and over time you will find that it grows into a steady warm fire, which will enable you to write more and more as you go through your life. The heat of the fire will become so strong and the light glowing from it will become so intense that all the critics will stand far away for fear of getting burnt or blinded. So Denise, appreciate the journeys you and your spark will go on and enjoy watching it grow.

Lots of love,

Denise

APPENDIX II
'HOUSE OF THE WRITERLY SELF' BY DENISE SAMARI

'You need to visit the House of your Writerly Self,' Bethany said.

'Where on earth is that?' I asked.

'Well every writer has one. But you need to draw it first and then you will know where to find it. When you have drawn it, you can visit it whenever you need to. Beware! Don't neglect it! If you do, some of the creatures will run amok.'

I drew my house and put it away in a drawer for several months. Then one day, when I was completely stuck with my storyline I decided to visit it. I took the plan of my house out of the drawer, and turning it over saw a map on the other side of the paper. There were words scrawled across the top: 'Start your quest by the light of a full moon, by the pool of silvery wonder, in the woods at the high gate.'

So, here I was, two days later, following the map, treading the trail that led to the house of my Writerly Self.

I glimpsed the house through the slim tree trunks. It was a huge Georgian affair with elegant sash windows. As I glanced at the façade, I saw that some of the windows were lit and then I heard a sound that sent tingles of fear trilling through my body. It was high-pitched, somewhere between a howl and a whine. It whipped around the house in a gush of air and stopped me dead in my tracks.

I looked up at the house again and then back at the dark moonlit track I had walked down. I wanted to go back. Never mind exploring those rooms! They could wait for someone else. 'That house and those rooms only belong to you,' said the voice in my head, in a tone that sounded worryingly like Bethany.

I hesitated on the path, torn between turning back and moving forward, when I noticed a face at one of the windows that looked familiar. I looked again. He had dark hair curling around his shoulders and a beard. A sequinned cap sparkled on his head. My heart skipped a beat: it was Habib, one of my main characters from the book I've been working on.

He saw me standing there and beckoned me with his finger. The howling continued but then I heard another sound. My characters singing the oneness song that I had written for them. They were singing loudly, trying to outdo the howling. I knew what I had to do then. I had to find my characters and help them. They were in trouble, they needed me.

* * *

The door to the house opened easily and I found myself in a big hall with a sweeping staircase up to the first floor. That was where I needed to go, that was where I had seen Habib. I ascended the stairs with trepidation. There was very little light and I could hear the howling floating down towards me, so that the higher I got, the louder it became.

Once at the top, I faced a long corridor running the

length of the house. It was dark, but I could see light glimmering out from underneath the closed doors. Now which room held my characters?

I bravely put one foot in front of another and walked along the corridor. The howling abruptly stopped and all of a sudden a terrible stench hit me. I looked to the left and saw a door wide open with the light of several candles on tables illuminating a ghastly apparition.

A being sat on a chair in the centre of the room. He resembled a kind of spider, with a face like a squashed rotten apple, but with a long pointy nose that stuck out in front of him and wiggled. He had six spindly legs, each one about six foot long, and on the end of each leg was something that looked like a crab's claw with pincers, that snapped open and shut continuously. I stood staring at him in shock. He looked at me with a smirk.

'So you think you can venture into the house of your Writerly Self. There is no room for you here. Get back to where you came from!' he hissed. 'When I have finished with this house, it will be little more than an abandoned shell. Then I will move on into the houses of others' dreams.' He laughed and extended his snapping claw towards me.

I ran from him to the nearest door. I could hear my characters singing behind it. I tried the handle. It was firmly shut. The creature was now standing in his doorway, two of his legs curling around the door frame, towards me. I banged on the door with all my might.

'Let me in!' I cried in desperation. The door opened and I collapsed into Habib's arms as the twins shut the door firmly on the creature.

'It's okay, you are safe now,' Habib reassured me.

'Thank goodness you are here. We've been waiting for you.'

'Have you? Why did you lock the door then?' I asked.

'Because we need to keep the monster out. He tries to get in at every opportunity. His name is Self-Doubt. In the early days we didn't realise how bad he could be, his smell wasn't as terrible and we were polite and tried to make friends with him. We invited him to take tea with us.

'At first it was just little things, words that were slightly barbed, insinuations that began to erode our self-confidence. Then he started to get serious, told us we weren't real, just a figment of our Creator's imagination. Even now when we keep the door locked and don't let him in, he still finds a way to get at us. He whines down the chimney, shakes the door in its frame and rattles the windows.

'We started to feel worn down by his constant nagging and it really got bad for some of us.' He gestured with his hand to the far corner of the room and I saw a huge cat the size of a panther, sleeping on a cushion.

'Yeruba!' I gasped.

'He has been asleep for a week now and his pulse is getting weaker,' Habib said. 'Self-Doubt told him he was preposterous, and that it was inconceivable that any sane reader would believe in him. He was already feeling sad since the last book ended with no news of what had happened to his best friend, Sartoshee.'

'But he has nine lives,' I said. 'I think he has one more left.'

Habib looked at me sadly. 'He has one left in the story but not here, not here in the house of your Writerly Self.

Here Self-Doubt, if not brought under control, has the power to kill any of us off.'

He clapped his hands suddenly. 'But where are my manners? You must meet the rest of the characters. What a joyful day this is! Our Creator has come to meet us.' The twins, Yashteen, Nadia and some of the other minor characters from my story came to greet me. They bowed formally and some of them took my hand and kissed it. I smiled and murmured some encouraging words, but I was wondering where my protagonists were.

'Where are Saffi, Fareed and Lilly?' I asked Habib.

'They are working for you. They have gone on a story-gathering mission to the Room of Imagination & Sparkly Magic. Harmony, Destan and Josh are in there too, trying to work out what happens next in Book Two. We've noticed you've stopped writing and we've all been very worried. You see this is how Self-Doubt gets to us. First he kills us off and then he works on you too. So they are trying to help by getting new ideas for you.'

'Where are my villains, Bajence, Oliah and Azmeer?' I asked.

'Come, I will show you.' I followed him up a spiral staircase to a round room full of books with walls full of maps. 'This is the Information Room. In here you can find maps of Perabar, books on its history, geography, styles of dress, cuisine, magic. Any background information you need about your story is in here.'

'So why are they in here then?' I nodded to where Bajence sat, his head immersed in a book, Oliah stroked her language bird, Shamleek, and Azmeer sat sullenly in a corner.

Habib dropped his voice to a whisper. 'They are trying to work out how they can add further destruction to Perabar. Behold!' He shouted out, 'Your Creator is here! Come and offer her homage!' Bajence glanced up from his book with a look of bored indifference and Oliah carried on stroking her bird, her gaze on some faraway point that no else could see.

Azmeer got up from his corner and came over; his fingers glowed like fluorescent light strips. 'I'm tired of being the bad guy,' he said.

'Maybe you need to rephrase that,' Habib said. 'Try asking nicely for a change.'

Azmeer looked at me and his steely grey eyes bore into me like light bulbs. 'Oh Great Creator,' he said in a sarcastic tone, 'I am sorry for my behaviour. But it's not my fault. You have made me this way. It's hard to change when I have been written to behave badly.'

'Nonsense!' shouted Habib. 'You had chances along the way.'

But I felt a nugget of sadness for Azmeer as he skulked back to his corner. If I get out of this situation in one piece, then I will try to help him in Book Two. Maybe.

We walked back downstairs. 'How can I defeat Self-Doubt?' I asked.

'We have a plan. You need to take the twins with you.'

'The twins,' I spluttered. 'How on earth can they help me? They will be more trouble than it's worth.'

'It is true, they do manage to get into the most ridiculous scrapes, but you saw how they helped to fight against Bajence in the first book. They are eager for adventure and need to prove themselves. They hope for a better role in your second book.'

When the twins saw us back in the room, they rushed over to my side and I looked at them doubtfully. At the corner of Arash's tunic I saw the gash of scar tissue and remembered how brave he had been when Azmeer was throwing his weapons of light at him. He saw me looking and said, 'I have faced a tempest of fire and made it through, I can face the monster who goes by the name of Self-Doubt.'

'Okay,' I said, 'so tell me your plan.'

Arash pulled a bouquet of flowers out from under his cloak and waved them under my nose. A heavenly scent of orange blossom, roses, jasmine and lilac filled the room. 'We will have to mask his sickening smell first.'

Next Ashkan sang up into the ceiling and three butterflies flew down and landed on his shoulder. 'This is Verdext,' he said, showing me the Technicolor Butterfly. 'He will distract and perplex Self-Doubt by fluttering in his face. This is Quastran,' he said, 'who will tickle him with his many wings by fluttering over his six legs, and this is Angeel, who will calm him by her beautiful presence.'

'Then,' said Habib, 'once he is calm, you can talk to him. It is possible that once he stops running around on his six legs and sticking his long nose into other people's business he might have something constructive to say, but he needs to learn how to be polite.'

We left Habib to look after Yeruba and entered the darkened corridor. A shadowy figure slipped out of Self-Doubt's room and rushed over to us. I flattened myself against the wall as he hurried over to me. He had a trilby hat on and a long raincoat. In his hands was a notebook and pencil. He strode over to me and barked, 'You know the middle of the story is nonsense, and why did you decide to make a creature like Sartoshee? Wasn't it enough to have a cat that changed into a man? Why did you need an eagle too?'

I stared at him stupefied, my stomach churning. Who was this obnoxious man? He leant towards me and his breath smelt of stale cigar smoke. 'Well!' he barked. 'I need your answers!' He had his notebook and pencil poised to write things down.

'I … er … well … I'm not sure …'

'No!' shouted the twins. 'Don't answer him. If you answer Inner-Critic, Self-Doubt grows bigger. That is what you have been doing. Somehow he gets out of the house and into your head. Never ever answer his questions and never read his reviews. Be gone, Inner-Critic! Back to the dark attic from whence you came!' and they sang a spell and waved their fingers over him.

He disappeared in a puff of smoke. I breathed a sigh of relief. I made a mental note to learn to recognise Inner-Critic, and to learn the spell that made him disappear. I thought, things are getting bad if he is running loose. I really need to check up on the house of my Writerly Self more often. No wonder I've had writer's block with all this going on.

We crept down the corridor to Self-Doubt's room. The smell leaked out towards us and Arash pulled his bouquet out. The doors were wide open and we turned and faced Self-Doubt. He sat on his chair in the centre of the room and he smirked with pleasure when he saw us. 'The useless twins,' he shouted 'You think you will amount to something! You need to stop trying now!' Then he looked at me. 'The Creator herself. You must stop trying! You will never ever be good enough. Inner-Critic and I have plans for you!'

'Don't listen to him!' the twins said, and they each took one of my hands. Then Ashkan talked to his butterflies and the plan unfolded. Verdext fluttered in his face and Quastron floated over his long legs, until he was a quivering jelly-like mess, heaving, spluttering and giggling on the floor. Then the beautiful Angeel with her large green wings and sedate manner floated over and perched on the edge of the chair. He looked at her serene being and was instantly calm. I knew this was my moment to talk to him.

'Look, Self-Doubt,' I said. 'You've got out of control. You've grown too big and are sticking your nose into all my characters' storylines. It's my fault I've let you grow like this. I should have come to the house more often. I've let my characters down, I've let me down. But you have to understand, my story *needs* to be written and I'm not going to let you or anyone else stand in my way.'

'But no one listens to me,' he wailed. 'No one wants to be my friend.'

'That's because you scare people. You make them doubt that they are real. Yeruba is seriously sick now because of what you've been telling him.'

'He didn't need to listen, it's not my fault he believed it,' he huffed.

'I don't think you can help me or my story,' I said.

As I uttered those words he started to shrink. He got smaller and smaller until he was the size of an octopus and suddenly I felt a presence behind me. I turned and there stood Yeruba in the form of a man. His long dark hair spread over his shoulders and the dark lines tattooed into his skin.

'Yeruba!' we gasped. He looked at me with his startling clear blue eyes.

'Thank you,' he said. He took my hands. 'Thank you for creating me. Thank you for making me real.'

I turned back to Self-Doubt. 'If you have something constructive to say I will listen, but I will only listen for five minutes. I think I know how all this started. It's because you were trying to protect me and you didn't want me to get hurt. I just listened for too long and I let you take over. You can still have a room in the house but it will be much smaller. Also, if you are polite, courteous and let others have a chance to talk, then my characters will occasionally invite you to tea. Oh, and I don't really think you need to consort with Inner-Critic.'

I left the house with my characters waving me off and a big bag bulging with stories collected by Fareed, Lilly and Saffi. I promised them I would be visiting a lot more often, and would never let things get so out of control again. As I skipped down the path, I felt a glow of excitement inside me, and felt ready and happy to start writing once more.

APPENDIX III
FUNDAMENTAL FEARS AND DESIRES

PERSONALITY	FEAR	DESIRE
Reformer	Of being 'bad', defective, evil or corrupt	To be good, virtuous, in balance, to have integrity
Helper	Of being unloved and unwanted for themselves alone	To feel loved
Achiever	Of being worthless, without value apart from their achievements	To feel worthwhile, accepted and desirable
Individualist	Of having no identity, no personal significance	To find themselves and their significance, to create an identity out of their inner experience
Investigator	Of being helpless, useless, incapable	To be capable and competent
Loyalist	Of having no support and guidance, of being unable to survive on their own	To find security and support
Enthusiast	Of being deprived and trapped in pain	To be happy, satisfied, to find fulfilment
Challenger	Of being harmed or controlled by others, of violation	To protect themselves, to determine their own course in life
Peacemaker	Of loss and separation; of annihilation	To maintain their inner stability and peace of mind

Table informed by *The Wisdom of the Enneagram: Complete Guide to Psychological and Spiritual Growth for the Nine Personality Types* by Don Richard Riso and Russ Hudson

FURTHER READING

Books and Collections

Bird by Bird: Instructions on Writing and Life – Anne Lamott, Bantam Doubleday Dell Publishing, 1980

Diving into the Wreck: Poems 1971–1972 – Adrienne Rich, Norton, 1973

Dream Work – Mary Oliver, Atlantic Monthly Press, 1994

On Writing: A Memoir of the Craft – Stephen King, Hodder & Stoughton, 2000

River Flow: New & Selected Poems – David Whyte, Many Rivers Press, 2012

The Artist's Way: A Course in Discovering and Recovering Your Creative Self – Julia Cameron, McMillan, 1992

The Hero with a Thousand Faces – Joseph Campbell, New World Library, 1949

The Right to Write – Julia Cameron, Penguin Putnam, 1998

The Seven Basic Plots: Why We Tell Stories – Christopher Booker, Continuum, 2004

The True Secret of Writing – Natalie Goldberg, Atria Books, 2013

The Wisdom of the Enneagram: The Complete Guide to Psychological and Spiritual Growth for the Nine Personality Types – Don Richard Riso and Russ Hudson, Bantam USA, 1999

The Writer's Journey: Mythic Structure for Writers – Christopher Vogler, Michael Wiese Production, 1992

Three Steps on the Ladder of Writing – Helene Cixous, Columbia University Press, 1994

Wild Iris – Louise Glück, W.W. Norton & Co., 1996

Writing Down the Bones (Freeing the Writer Within) – Natalie Goldberg, Shambhala Publications, 1986

You Do Not Need Another Self-Help Book – Sarah Salway, Pindrop Press, 2012

Poems

'Autobiography in Five Short Chapters' – Portia Nelson

'Beannacht' – John O'Donohue

'Digging' – Seamus Heaney

'The Fountain' – Denise Levertov

'The Guest House' – Jalaluddin Rumi, translated by Coleman Barks

'The Way It Is' – William Stafford

'Thirteen Ways of Looking at a Blackbird' – Wallace Stevens

'Thirteen Ways of Looking at a Poet' – Lesléa Newman

"Poetry" – Pablo Neruda

TED Talks

Brené Brown – https://www.ted.com/talks/brene_brown_on_vulnerability?language=en

Elizabeth Gilbert – https://www.ted.com/talks/elizabeth_gilbert_on_genius?language=en

Websites

Cheryl Richardson – http://www.cherylrichardson.com/store/take-time-for-your-life-introduction/

Audio Books

The Creative Fire: Myths and Stories About the Cycles of Creativity by Clarissa Pinkola Estes (1993) (mp3s/CDs)

About the Author

Bethany Rivers' debut pamphlet, *Off the wall*, was published by Indigo Dreams Publishing. Her second poetry collection *the sea refuses no river* is being published by Fly on the Wall Press, due out 21st June 2019. Her biggest passions in life are writing and enabling others to write.

Bethany Rivers' novel *The Virgin & The Whore* was published by Vanguard Press. She has been widely published in poetry magazines, anthologies and online in the UK and USA, including Fly on the Wall Press, Envoi, Cinnamon Press, Bare Fiction, Fair Acre Press, Verve Poetry Press, Yorkshire Valley Press, Silver Birch Press, The Lampeter Review, The Lake, Blithe Spirit, High Window Literary Journal, Laldy Scottish Literary Journal, Writers' Cafe, Riggwelter, I am not a silent poet, Picaroon Poetry, Three Drops from a Cauldron, The Ofi Press.

She has an M.A. in Creative Writing from Cardiff University and has taught creative writing for over 13 years. She also mentors writers individually, through the writing of their novels, short stories, children's fiction, memoirs, and poetry: www.writingyourvoice.org.uk

Bethany Rivers is also editor of the online poetry magazine, *As Above So Below,* which publishes poetry on the theme of spirituality and transcendence.

Acknowledgements

Many thanks to everyone at Victorina Press for all their hard work. I'd like to thank all my students, throughout the years. It's been a privilege to get to know you and your work, and be witness to your flourishing relationships with words. This book wouldn't have been possible without you. Special thanks to Hannah Hull for the illustrations. And thanks to David Stevens. I'd especially like to thank Denise Samari and Geraint Jones as well as all the loyal followers of my Poetry Inspiration Days. Thanks also to Cerys.